MW01381532

Canada Post

Jason Christie

SNARE BOOKS . MONTREAL . 2006

Copyright © 2006 by Jason Christie

All rights reserved. No part of this publication may be reproduced, stored in a retrieval system or transmitted, in any form or by any means without the prior written permission of the publisher.

Edited and Designed by Jon Paul Fiorentino
Copyedited by derek beaulieu
Typeset in Minion

NATIONAL LIBRARY OF CANADA CATALOGUING IN PUBLICATION DATA

Christie, Jason, 1977-
Canada post / Jason Christie.

Poems.
ISBN-13: 978-0-9739438-0-1
ISBN-10: 0-9739438-0-7

1. Nationalism--Canada--Poetry. I. Title.

PS8555.H719C35 2006 C811'.6 C2006-901204-0

Printed and bound in Canada

Represented in Canada by the Literary Press Group
Agented by Conundrum Press

SNARE BOOKS
784 Laurier Ave E.
Montreal, Quebec
H2J 1G1

Canada Post

PAST ORAL
i. Metathesis

PAST AURAL
i. anamnesis suite

PAST ORAL
ii. Revelry.Correspondences

PAST AURAL
ii. short terse poems

PAST ORAL
iii. Spring Tension

PAST AURAL
iii. neutrino (means little one)

PAST ORAL
iv. Make Fire

PAST AURAL
iv. swerve

PAST ORAL
v. An Emotional Database

For Joyce and Beulah

A hi-fi system is one possessing a favourable signal to noise ratio. The hi-fi soundscape is one in which discrete sounds can be heard clearly because of the low ambient noise level. The country is generally more hi-fi than the city; night more than day; ancient times more than modern. In a hi-fi soundscape even the slightest disturbance can communicate interesting or vital information.

R. Murray Schaffer, 'The Music of the Environment.'

In a lo-fi soundscape individual acoustic signals are obscured in an overdense population of sounds.

R. Murray Schaffer, 'The Music of The Environment.'

i. Metathesis

The poem put us into battle. Language versus. A landscape emerges amongst the words, nations between the letters, earths the pristine page into your heart's content: Let mud slowly bleed into the poem's veins. Nature verses. X equals a jetty, an extension of the nation into the sea, a skeleton, a linebreak, scaffold, land, gift, an address, a title, a deed. Keep me safe from the poem. As though it rained. Rain.

If by a lake, then your body becomes a buoyant container for words, floats through paragraphs, past sentences; my geographic insistence maps a typology necessitated by depression and height; my letterform perspective presses a hunger pang of elevation in my belly, forms letters, a sentence in the page — A sleepless verb moves through the air, pushes into ink. Weather is a verb or a multiple gesture unrealizable within a system determined by capital, currency, within a writing:

A RAINSTORM WILL COST YOU A FORTUNE

You always smile when the clouds darken from white to gunmetal grey, the blue from your eyes, blue in a sunshine ring. Your arms reassemble a promise from bits of wool, water flits from my shoulders, falls to the ground, slicks off my wings. Love and nations are multiple. Neither can make it rain.

Make it rain. Let me, I said, be defined as a container, a lake. Water pools but does not constitute geographical importance enough for a name on a map. Land forms in lines there. I'm landlocked in the reality of a poem where water is mythic. Water multiplies outward from a raindrop in a lake; one lands or plots a zero surrounded by trees. The autumnal economy or poem rolls fiery into the hills, an elevated depression, a south-western Ontario escarpment, flattened landforms represented topographically by lines in dreams on paper, a written language writing me.

LANGUAGE AS A NATIONAL EVENT (RAIN REPRISE)

A nation guards against loneliness. A nation excludes you, it is a container, a lake, a geography. A nation escapes photographs. Our national weather united in the forecast. The poem descends from an elevation just above sea-level, it costs us our nation and it promises rain. Makes promises. It rains.

This poem isn't a nation. A nation of trees pulped and bleached into something we are bound to recognize through the ink, through the words. Think through:
1. Your right to watch The Simple Life is a guarantee.
2. There are doors in the walls of your nation which can be locked, the blinds on the windows drawn, shutters closed, a mapped carpet covers the trap door in the living room of your nation. Only you and I know about it now.
3. This nation is not a poem at war.
4. There are no more trees in this poem.
5. The nation mourns.
6. The presidency locates itself outside the poem.
7. The nation used to be a ritual.
8. The poem was a small house in the country near some sheep.
9. The poem used to be a body.
10. A nation is no longer invisible.
11. Little children run around the poem playing 'nation' until dusk.
12. Our lockable nation organizes around necessity. To keep the bugs out, it has screens on all the windows and doors, to keep the animals beyond what we built, there are walls and fences around the nation, to keep food on the table we spell words correctly; we sleep well at night all wrapped up in our nation. Who will speak for this poem?

22 STATEMENTS ABOUT A FEAR OF BEING ALONE (OR EXISTENTIALISM) IN THE DARK

1. Technology always operates in the service of humanity.

2. Science could be defined as human intelligence applied in the process of determining the world through representation: Numbers, diagrams which approximate reality, hypotheses, observations, a collective project, conclusions or as an extension of religious sovereignty.

3. The assumption that language is a cogent system for transmitting information is fraudulent at best.

4. The scientific process enables technological innovation: Refinement plus improvement with the goal of perfection. Words to live by.

4b. Of perfection: The sentence aspires, always aspires. I aspirate.

5. A: By which scale? What rules? Can I get a pamphlet about this?

6. Every diagram tells the same truth: The machine doesn't ever hug you back.

7. Communication combines fascism and illusion. We listen. You read. Did I say Communication? I meant to say technology. Do you know what I mean?

8. Asleep on the wall, you hear a story about gravity and the world tilts you to the floor. There is comfort in incorrect knowledge too. The sun sets, I have a diagram to explain how the sun sets.

9. Comprehend an assembly line.

10. Q: Ideology is not entirely accurate. Innovate at my expense.

11. Toasters are mirrors for your desire. I want to tell you something.

12. What perpetually draws meaning away from the necessity of its transmission is as terrorism is to the United States or a pulsar to its accreting disk. Who is wrong and what are we missing when we choose to choose sides? What does a non-utilitarian machine look like?

13. Q: Capable of love? A: Dispassionately.

14. I wanted to tell you about flowers. Language operates in the service of humanity.

14b. I'm an operator in the service of technology.

15. Knife like. Like life. Flight!

16. Non-reciprocating bodies involve a gaze of possession and creation applied to bodies capable of reciprocation when considered as non-reciprocating by the subject administering the gaze. For example, when I say "You are an object and you look angry" (as opposed to anthropomorphism), I tell you stones can cry. Stones are non-reciprocating bodies. But you probably still shouldn't throw them at glass houses.

17. Be careful about reading a wooden figure, splatter of ink or pile of clay into something you'll have to live with. Your desire creates others (as in how best to serve toasters).

18. I'll show you my source code if you'll show me yours. I'll show you my bastardized teleology. Innovate with my expense account for your leisure.

19. The movie 2001 proposes that artificial intelligence will understand errors as the result of clumsy human interference and will take action to eradicate the source of its error. Technology always operates in the service of humanity. The movie Blade Runner proposes that machines will seek to understand their creator, and ultimately eclipse Him. Science as an elaborate myth.

20. Q: What is comforting about what is?

21. When machines attack versus when machines choose not to attack.

22. There is nothing, then there is something and you are not as alone as you felt previously. Scratch that. There is everything, then you select something and feel less alone than you felt before. Which of these sentences is incorrect?

22b. A: So, just tell me already.

i. anamnesis suite

CANDOR (THE END)

erse flush
against flush,
track attract, dear
they ought to plumb
each writ, frozen
tree, a nick, deli
elbow, word
button or arrow, a
lever, l ver, shush, eh?,
o you, i
be leaf you,
my th ng,
i w sh
a st r
. period

GAME VS. REAL

There are typos
all over the word.

REHEARSAL

Ideas erstwhile heap.
He leaped sound.
Asleep at her feet.
A traffic able attic.
Track tacit static.
Tree points plot things.
As a rehearsal for words.

This is what happens during the poem:

1. You come home.
2. You sit on my lap.
3. I'm talking on the telephone.
4. It is a friend of mine.
5. You walk to the kitchen to wash celery.
6. Our neighbours slam their door again.
7. I have a shower and crawl into bed beside you.

IMÀGE

Night bells slay
the hear or heard
of language. Rain,
dear, the very
meaning of you, just
the very meaning of you
is the unsled of snow;

a salient lingua
in the moonlight.

WING NUT

Screw the
original, an
unpunctuated
forest for
the trees. A
cabinet or taxi
ride downtown.
Screw the copy
of photographic
quality, I'm
going to bed
and so am I.

ii. Revelry.Correspondences

And I thought: My god says there's heat lightning all over our alpha bits this morning. The telephone wasn't for you. We asked for a receipt earlier because we wanted it in writing that our meal could withstand a Western audit. Heard you voted Tory in the last federal election. Well, I'm squatting right now in the middle of the poem, and if you leave your name and phone number after the beep I will be sure to get back to you as soon as possible. And I checked the lease and thought: My god, ten dollars is a reasonable price to pay for breakfast with you, the mood suddenly lightening between us under the oppressive heat. The little bit between Aleph and Omega-3 fatty acids. Someone called about our high speed Internet account while you were in the shower. I told them it would probably rain.

Storms overheard, a rain of footsteps stampedes across the roof, drops shepherded by the wind to splatter the skylight. An alpha unfolds through the bolt on the door in the archaeology of the moment, and wind gets into the home. I bet the fastener gets wet outside, beyond the letter sea, wear a scarf in perpetuity, an A, or an R forever. Our hands, when they finally touch, invent the rest of the alphabet, chemical designs in our sweat, words, a map revealed in the sounds and smells between our bodies, a language: The universe listens. And I thought: My god, I'd buy you a semi-detached home somewhere in the newly developed neighbourhoods of the poem, near water. Heard you didn't vote in the last municipal election. Well, hell, Romania wasn't built in an arbitrarily defined period anyway. Anyway, period

You are an I-memory, a magical mirror, a "wish image" warrior, or an armored mirage. Things thin blood, a body broods and wastes an abode: Bees in honeycombs in boxes in yards to birds in trees or names in taxonomies, to list 'em slow-like, to mow the lawn, to smoke 'em from their boxes, the best, the beesknees. Letters in the archive, letters to, and form gifts: love becomes the sum of an archaism.

I saw some fish swim in the cobalt waters of the Athabasca River near Mt. Christie on the West side of Glacier Parkway. Wind, green trees, pine needles, circles age out sap. Watch my honey glaze. Sure, my arms reach into the moraine lake valley. Valley, valley oxygen fee with nobody home. Roads follow arched shale fossil records. Height pines: Thin thing, a graph, a ph of 0, with no down pavement, a good night's sleep on my new limestone crouch with or without my drought and a pill or two in the ditch upon which to rest my head and shoulders, knees and toes. My hands indebted across the word America — a ghost stretched there for clarity. Please, don't mention it again. Sprinkles of rain conjoin discrete provinces, drops sizzle behind cars. Sign here along the yellow dotted line or just drive. I dent if I fall over the white median too. Interstates of license and registration slip and freeze. Dynamic inroads flood then still; the poem becomes a sequence of grifts where you move your wallet to, and then you move there too.

You might have reservations even though the poem spreads and cools without you. You'll have an idea, a cirque or a silver ribbon in a semi-circular box wrapped with red paper. Smooth rocks revealed in the early Spring runoff from the mountains. We're throwing stones across the terminal moraine forever alongside Glacier Parkway in a blizzard on April 14th, 2002. Natural formations of record melt and freeze and freeze in several directions at once, then Slip. These things are glyphs, are gifts. Slip. I'm in your hands now. Slip

Am I too locally referential or too diachronically interstitial to be alone at home? To be, then, understood requires another level for the other. Understand? What in the hell does that mean? That (tht, tht) n. pl. those (thz): A rare bird with bold green plumage and International Klein Blue feet believed to have inspired musicians for centuries and such classic songs as 'My life in particle physics.' Khaki like H Street like kickball. I'm in that picture near the window and you are framed over there by the door. Rob birds and fly with fire. Sell xenophobia. Spell asphyxia. Pull the word apart to toffee in your warm hands, then spread them wide and cover yourself with feathers. R-I-G- -T? Put on your metal shirt. There will be legal proceedings on the second floor. Just be patient, and I'll doctor the forms right away so that you are in the picture when I get to the door. Don't you judge me. I just want to be loved. The Beaufort Sea brings 'us' closer together than Uranium-decay diagrams. Feel free to calibrate the letters however you see the Romantic fit. Insert tab A into wing slot B, then fly. I seek you. Calvin Klein would say: "The space allowed by the bridge contains many places variously near or far from the bridge. These places, however, may be treated as mere positions between which there lies a measurable distance; a distance, in Greek stadion, always has room made for it, and indeed by bare positions. The space that is thus made by positions is space of a peculiar sort. As distance or 'stadion' it is what the same word, stadion, means in Latin, a spatium, an intervening space or interval. Thus nearness and remoteness between men and things can become mere distance, mere intervals of intervening space. In a space that is represented purely as spatium, the bridge now appears as a mere something at some position, which can be occupied at any time by something else or replaced by a mere marker." It doesn't really matter. I still miss you. My tears are as sturdy as your ankles. Place my image along the Niagara Escarpment somewhere and then your eyes in relation to it. Et Voix-la! Where is your reader? I am right here on the other side of the Canadian Shield. It would be nice to spend a day in the glyphs. Here, this, sun, shine

Thunder is the sound of a linebreak. A sentence flashes in half and closes. The night folds. The night folds under pressure from the paragraph to standardize language and incorporate meaning; we annex darkness to daylight and say of it: "O the folds of a rose fold like night." Just try and time the semantic back-and-forth to deliver a message with slightly more currency than when it was sent to you. Read all about it! A cross arrives across a river, a game set in points, a horn undone by progress. Of the future: write an epilogue about the books within which we live and then turn out the light when you leave. What tremors between capital and periods? Empires quietly develop in our hearts as we learn to appreciate marks and aspire toward intellectual sovereignty, then we wait as dusty pages rest in books ached to engage again with readers, with subjects. Your heart beats on the shelf, thunder claps and then rolls over our homes. I've affixed the past into the top right corners of nostalgia, adjacent to what became of telegrams and letter carriers. Drop me a line when you can, send me a poem into the eventual limit of a busted and abused market, build me a nation less like a pine tree but more neon so that I can sleep better tonight wrapped in blanks, in the spaces between words, where we all eventually rest, silence between the paragraph and the presidency, reset blankets and startle my arms around you. I don't want to be alone. Click send.

Every autumn expands the GAP nested between my age and my shoe size. Let snow cover my begonias and the GNP — hey, it isn't excessive to throw your old breast implants into the Bow River for golden retrievers to fetch. Poetry, she said to me over some pinot noire and goose liver paté in the hospitality suite at the Palliser, is a niche market (well, thanks, I replied, I just had it stuffed). Tiny industry, read this between the lines of your indecipherable subway map: You perpetually win my hand, my lance, and my last lonely advance from the last forest milieu into the city. I'll trade your employees for a messy famine. Letter by letter, word by word, and sentence by sentence, avant! — either the snow falls or you win again (rhymes with bread, out for a walk, served with fancy mustard, you can thank Williams, junior, for that one). Pass some sourdough or rye and I'll switch subway lines (take Capitalism to work or we'll drive on through to the next American whiskey bar). The poem started an investment company on the Internet called The Book (really, though, it was more of a corporation that traded in futures). Step into the offices of the poem when the snow falls, fall into the snow office at the next full stop in the poem, stop by our office because there is no top floor to the poem and we need a janitor to clean the elevator. I'll levitate, or press the buttons on your coat against the chill winter wind, wind up your watch, watch it or I'll tighten your muffler, or I'll do that for you too, because, quite frankly, between you and me, your car makes an awful noise screeching between floors. Love, - 15, let me put it this way: Don't scarf down your blueberry pancakes before tennis lessons or you'll get indigestion and make a horrible racket. Gamble away the net profits of your little nation at the Worldwide Poker Championships held on the 11th Floor of the new WTO building. In my country, there are always more where it came from anyway (myth). Anyway, tell someone how your starry sky falls into a spring. Fiery poems settle, reflected in a monolith of dark windows. Tear them all down into light

I don't have anything. I import an ant to say. A witch is as much a critique of the GAP as it is rain against the moonroof. Fluency spins under low grey clouds, lonely, it anthropomorphizes as whatever animal got into the trash last night. There were banana peels all over the sidewalk this morning. And one drunk raccoon. Probably the same that stole your panties from the laundry line in our backyard, the laundry line upon which you had clipped pages and photographs of your underwear to dry after our basement flooded. Little poems like flipbooks where stick figures fall through the gender hole in the floor. Quick turn the page. Turn the page into a Manitoban border guard at the top of a ladder. A sentence blurs two weeks in advance of the letter S meant to introduce fisheries into the Calgary economic structure then devolves into a vole that voluntarily evolved vulgar and garish trackpants. But I do want a new microwave or maybe a new mastoid process or at the very least an Alberta to go bang bang to the boogie to the boogie to the Bow river to be.

The letter folds from corner to corner into a swan that bursts forth from the sinewy narrative of an ugly duckling turned porn king. Get thee two nunneries or at least an attractive fishery worker if any can be found among the masses. Sometimes [pause] when I try to sleep I see your face clearly, smiling, with one eyebrow slightly raised, an upside down V, your beautiful smile [record] fades.

I've got your digits stuck in my blackberry. Your name ceases to resonate below a certain level of yellow crabgrass. Say, we'll call you lawn. Now you're mowed under a reference to a picture of my grandparents' backyard before they had the build-a-better-back-porch war with the neighbors to the south. There are lots of characters caught in sand dunes, and, then, when it rains in the novel, the trenches fill with mud and water. The legend implies an army or two near Hastings. Blasted, half a year gone before the calendar can catch up and I've barely told you about my new computer. Well, that's the way the words organize themselves, not in a line, but as a universe spelled linearly with a whimper. Why bang a simple skyscraper?

Sort of like we were in one conversation, then it rained, and now we're talking about cars over coffee at Higher Ground. There is no narrative tension. It is all in my head. So why remember that a change around the house is as good as an arrest? Build that bookshelf instead. Don't build that bookshelf instead. When you said it rained, did you mean like Queen Victoria and I just heard the typo? My epistolary uncle Harry called right in the middle of May to justify my laziness. My pistol-leery uncle Larry called homonyms heterosexist propaganda during the peace march last April. He might ask you to bring deviled eggs to his 50th birthday party. And maybe a new car too. Now, I'm just trying to single out one cow from the herd. I don't remember whose phone number that is? This is simply pastoral. Send me an email, drop me a line, msn me, man. I wanted to tell you that in the end, my leg went to Japan and then I mailed my arm to Sicily for no particularly good reason.

Sugar in your gas tank these days, eh? Who could afford not to be rich? Or at least who could afford not to buy Vitamin C enriched peanut butter and milk? I'm at home in a First world kind of way tonight if you'd like to bring over some DVDs and cheap Italian wine.

I don't like checkers, but crown me a king anyway. Personally, I'd rather play poker than be all rabid in your head lice.

ii. short terse poems

DIPLOMACY

Have some
turkey with
sweet potatoes.

Now you and I
are conquerors.

This is our poem.

It is your profit margin
anyway, ya bastard.

LUNA PRESSURE

Order me half
a McResponsibility —
a fragile coke guardian
wanes to sleep.

We target boomers —
with can I help you?

Newly-waxed
machine suits
set to work, forms
filled to keep
business along new data lines.

Parental structures
or soccer moms fear
full minivans, keeps grids
rigid, call it "pleasure."

Call it pleasure

GALLOP POLL

Fuck off!

REAGANOMICS REPRISE

That's a pretty nice fabric. Ah
yeah, that's a pretty nice fabric.
A fabric: Yeah, that's pretty nice.
That's pretty nice fabric, yeah.
Ah, yeah, that fabric is pretty nice.

FREEZER

A nation of genuine millions,
united states of this array.
Relevance blossomed like eros.
The bridge between words
has been closed for weeks.
A walk in the inferential rain
derailed the refrain:
"it takes a village of nations
of genuine millions
to scratch our backs."

HERPES SOCK

"Rumour mill pulps
good intentions,"
the headlines proclaim.
And there is always
more news at eleven.

FOR BOTH BUSHES

The birds we dewhistled sing in heaven.

NOT A CIRCUMPOLAR TOUR IS

"Why,
Cancun is just like
1950's rural America!"

open $50
fold

ALPHABET POEM

You put the un
in unamerican.

iii. Spring Tension

SPRING TENSION: NOSTALGIC (FOR M)

An aphorism: A chrome for the blatant eme as per your mission. The attractive brown haired girl on the corner in the past wants to hold your slender hand as stars beat a path toward the nearest coffee shop to then sit on some concrete steps like a neon symbol of all that isn't even close to being wholly independent nor a true silver letter to skip metal over and cover a teeth clenched goodbye before the hairs on your neck shine then stand and shiver again then shine as though the air froze in the middle of summer and the ground shifted into a clause you stand on for at least a half an hour after she leaves to draw some pictures of an old building. Your own

Does the pomegranate cry seeds when we hold hands and our necks strain from meaning so well that we could shuffle away from any sense and from any sentence like a joker into the middle of a poker deck for six months of the year? Run away from lean prose. Good down to the last drop's course through the air; a period; a learned pose; an order: The wave tunnel closes itself after the full stop and opens before it into space at the same time per second per second. Sugar swirls up in a coffee cup, matter moves then dissolves, changes states, the onset of turbulence in a dynamic system, the v dissipates as aroma and resurfaces, convection in the local atmosphere like meaning and words into and out of attentive focus, or else those billboards again. She returns. She returns. She returns. She comes. Pan right. Star left. Pan right. She is coming. She is coming. She is

Like bark on a tree in the park. Trunk then bark some advantage to sunlight as it leaves and binds darkness into repetition. The bird's perch juts over the chasm. Aspen or birch, a curve dogs the ground, forces me (united in theory) down to why gravity is weaker than the forces inside atoms and between particles, drags the r into n (such a small distance to fall). "The look of extreme gravitas." Leashes theory and tethers letters. In other words: A grand string between the house and shed upon which to hang your wet laundry. A line, a lyre string strung out, caught tense like that past or pants on fire, we amble our way into the yard. Why is my dithyramb green? We drunkenly follow nouns into the sentence like fenceposts thrown into the street, and decide to take the car to keep pace. A rigid wall, standing wave, rain smashes into traffic. We see it approach through the windshield and put on our seatbelts. Something punctuates the ground. To turn a phrase still spends time. Glass or else grass

Vectors plot weather on your blackberry. A GPS system and poetics to keep the device together as if it falls apart, the world, captain leisure, sand grains and glass in your hands, stars, techné, letters and lines help you to picture this and to fall apart: The frame can go to your head or at least the chassis of your SUV. There are locations to donate, verdant hills and shores, a screen with swallows appears there, where they fly around you, printed on maps; charity shadows the windows. We close our shutters. Some paint, some canvass, to try. Birds and trees and taxonomies tidied up for you in a book. Picture this as you snap each rung of the hierarchy on your way down: My love in the folds of a flower or a ditch, I swear, is where there is a wood-hulled boat off the page away from the sun on some beach, imagine it drawn on canvas in blue, green and brown. Rumble, strum and chord your progress to avoid graphs in song; sonic geometry washes in and breaks on the overtones, beaks squawk around silence; the sand folds into noise and recedes from letters; the noise of grains lost in sound: information in a registry, a market forms. And we talk about it. Flag masts snap and flash golden into strength again and against the sirens, to say the least, art crashes desperately to the beach in search of a name, of love

iii. neutrino (means little one)

IMPOSSIBLY SHORT

drops a little rain
softness ‘around
the eyes’ salt
some wind
anyway

TEETH

Compound my daily interest,
baby wrench.

CHURCHBELLS IN SPACE

I've always wanted
to be a nihilist
but I really love
antiques.

True to type,
your robot dreams
about a noun.

TAN

Pillow a pull, ow!
Get the goose
doon!

HAPPY NEW YEAR(S)

I promise not
to smoke any
more than ten
cigarettes a day.

GANG BANG

To the city limit! The farmers
aid a pronoun's entrenchment
in the field. Hay turned
and tilled, the tilted word,
world-slid economic grid, now
that's entertainment, eh?

GENTLE SLOPE INTO BOOK

You be the person who sweeps
and I'll be the one who turns off
the lights at the end of the poem.

iv. Make Fire

Sounds like an arrangement to me. I'm afraid of emoticons. When did all the arrows change direction? I went to the bathroom and made it back to my seat in time for the credits, but forgot which movie we were here to see. I'll tell you all about it later. The bathrooms are over there. A polar bear, two pounds of hashish and a corncob pipe. What I mean to say is. There really isn't a difference between where you meant to get to and where you've ended up. Space. I just wanted to tell you that you have a really great asp. Put that in your back pocket and smoke it. I have the letter from the city to the forest around here somewhere. It said something like: you're fired. I bought this book on the Internet. Steppe 1: open wrapper. Steppe 2: destroy contents. Steppe 3: ? Steppe 4: I think we've really turned a corner here.

NEUTRINO (MEANS LITTLE ONE)

I am three letters. You are a new phenomenon. What it is. That's discord. My country advanced the page into a 21st century screened tamper-proof of logic: Unstable to appear there, a new generation built from "a thousand points of light," your new pet project: To monitor the plateaus. In vitro estimation of language to be then and just be then what is now is it. Directly rip, it barely reacts with any form of matter. Matter (comma) words.

SWERVE (GENTLE GRADE)

I pressed May flowers in a union book, and moved the story forward one hour. Our labour reps got the directions to the CN Tower wrong somewhere along the way or else they would have been here for our morning coffee break. Oh, are you new in the plot? Have some pain au chocolat and coffee. The main office is to the east near where a tired trench exists like some negative horizon, over there, off the page, beneath the flags in a gutter, a gully; I think I'm in a sentence near the margins. The point is perpetually not here. It is delayed along the line. Moved away. Like mad, clack, the black shapes sway back and forth, unreadable by any light, letters train behind words, fall, sway back and forth then fall, an autumnal book unreadable by any light, although, once understood, the track we talk becomes distressingly perceptible.

If I've told you once, I've told you a thousand times: Money through your wallet is not just paper thrown on the floor, it is not a was-green thing, doesn't justify the cost of pamphlets against a radical tree-form diagram strewn between cracks in the infrastructure (read sidewalk), plotlines written in red on green graph paper near the curb. We need to spend more time online. Money is an Escalade (and power) and now colourless. Epic stock portfolios regale young minds, dramatize acumen and bravado in business to those who know how to read such economic reports. Even if it is all you have left, your success will lull hundreds to sleep in the future the way stories used to, give it a squeeze. In the interview, I told.them you were right for the part. You're a character witness. Calliope finds tight platforms on high for you with the number one and a bunch of zeroes cross-legged amongst a pile of coins. Fill in your form for quiet then we'll have our people call your people. Thunder and wind, sad cloud. Rocks and rain. Now you then be here. Or over there. Or over here.

Call me in to work when you are sick. Spread thin down the steps and we won't know when you've crossed our neighbourly threshold. Don't stow your junk mail in our brickyard. Are you a forest person or a desert person? The letter A nomads through the local alphabet in search of water: A European hangup that is afraid of desertification. We built a bridge over sand in order to conjoin forests but what hides under our noses in the future milieu? Bagels contribute to an arid inheritance. I parked my SUV beside an Oak tree a thousand years ago but now I've lost it in the dunes and dust storms. Gee, I remember when everyone had a pool in their backyard.

SWERVE (STEEPER GRADE)

Rough music motivates our gentle recapitulated social need for norms and critics like Ebert and Roeper at the movies or Tucker Carlson. Who remembers Tucker Carlson? Won't someone please remember Tucker Carlson? Merry anger hides a great and elemental excavated and envious greed; it gleams green in our eyes. I'd like to watch the tower rise from the book, see the tree grow from inside the seed but I don't know why. I'd trade my kingdom for a horse whisperer. The trigger hairline like a Roy Kafka fight scene: a fracture but not so metallic as that revelry. O the rogering you could get. In my sense of life, the more judicious room grew fins, gills slit the walls, the ceiling resembles an immense ribcage and I saw a luminescent fish with bright orange and blue scales. It swam into my eyes and cut my hair, corresponded with my teeth, cut my teeth in the backyard, I cut my teeth for the first time in three weeks, three weeks and a charcoal portrait of a computer on the front cover. Close all the doors. Over there a deciduous has decided to decline into the book, was, will be, has been, would be, is being, is bent to the ground outside the window in invitation. Fall on the guards, guard my portfolio wisely, help me widen the gulf between poverty and poetry. I storm the keep and keep the letters assembled from the rain. They will say to me: "don't you dare go out alone tonight, or else."

But I might say of it: "I don't have enough money to conspire?" Instead of a frontier to best, my nation is a rumour we carved letter by letter into a land we found and then printed on maps in blue ink. Skin stretched over our bones. You and I thunder borders, and then lay down in the bay like an island that looks like a sleeping giant. Nations dissolve, sovereigns deposed, I settle as a victorious consumer, park the car and punch into home. Canada likes a monarchy. A digital breeze shudders standards across all the monitors. Extra! Extra! Letter carriers herald change: Nations organize in the wake of communication technologies' progress. Data lines reconfigure coordinates. Where do I work? My nation like weather comes home like rainstorms, shifts across the surface of the earth. My future doesn't need me now that I've built a new organism. Canada settles into the past, makes me as quaint as a royalist. Nations used to center on individuals, then on collectives, and now nations organize around points in a power grid, centers on transaction. Of flux: nodes in a matrix, they follow pulses and search for energetic aggregates; my body nomads through cities, my body acts as a house for a worker; poems or nations startle, shift and settle. I heard a rumour of fixed geographical boundaries and imagined it like a poem of the world I saw in a History book when I was younger. I might say of it: "But I never wanted a new hard drive even though I need one to join the union. I am Canadian." The difference is between my nation and an electric cattle fence in a snowstorm. Borders are political curtains. I'll close my windows. It might rain. I'll close my shutters. I'll stay in the living room. I'll stay bound by the light.

LURK (POEM FOR [MAILSNAIL])

Yellow leaves and enters autumn, that hesitant Georgian architecture forms a venerated space from words: A wet season we weather (the population determines itself in articulate and gentle advances of the idea that the Internet is a narrative. What we have here when what we have is nothing and the intense community of homes half-built into information, our city forms like this, aqueous and awkward, without actually taking place or shape, inside brackets, along the parenthetical line). Given a wind, we generate all of October, thankful at last for the ample vocalization of magnetism at the poles: Shiver for warmth until sunrise and I'll promise you some coffee to antagonize the soak from your bones.

The font remains unaccomplished. Glass or else grass or else a smashed punctuation intimated at within the sentence that contains it. Cars drive by. Night settles. And we drive by. An impossible rendition of clouds in music, an impossible font; I am afraid of the impetus empty frames suggest. Grass or else graveyard. In gravitas we trust. Too much to earth. A tomb marker maker. A little letter. A center to swing round swings a round upon the centre. Language puts us in to battle. Language verse. It contains. We lose. Words swim. It doesn't matter anymore. The font remains.

iv. swerve

AUCTORITAS

He makes a fire
and watches TV.

The headlines are
behind the times.

I waste it while
I watch it.

The USA created
the super power vacuum.

In order to feel secure
go stand in the light.

The child's box
is in the pen.

One of the seals
in my car leaks.

Penguins flew from
Pittsburgh to Toronto.

He helps an old lady
across to the GAP.

In order to feel secure
go stand on the right.

While in school
wear something reflective.

Even when you move
you never really unparse.

Learning to derive
is an automotive process.

Don’t end your sentence
with a preposition.

SEPSIS (A DIRTY POEM)

Ply rough, just
do it! Doggie
style of the stylus,
stylo against the grain
gains water levels
for your benefit.
Cough up piles.
The fur rug shines
ermine! Comb a victory

NOSTRIL INVERNESS

I've got WMD.
Let me explain:
I bought a universal
power adapter but
it won't help you.
Arched, aqueduct,
aquiline: paternal
discourse knows best.
The doctor said:
WMD usually
lasts 6-8 weeks.
Until then I'm supposed
to default to authority.

GNP

The worst part of peaches,
a female newscaster said,
are the spits. Armies asleep,
entrenched up to their eyeballs
in Schubert. Puckerhole roughs
the smooth psyche of the people,
call it memory, a sense, the ability
to remain profitable.

And a mountain's edge,
tectonic cleft trebles,
aeroscopic field notes,
play the flax landscape.
Bass viewed from a plane
sideways, or Charlie
syntagmatically drops
not a shift or a shrift, but
that keen target slides
for acumen, hides
whitehoused behind
missals or missives in
a bizarre cardboard box.

MAGNOLIA (LOTUS EATERS)

I'll bring the cordial
when binary code
goes capital;
how do you love
a profit machine?
My car for your kingdom,
ok? Poem. Ok,
[interlude]
Guitar Solos vs.
Bank Accounts —
don't walk out
on me again, hippie.

Circle us a ring
"das Ding en Sich!"

v. An Emotional Database

prologue. I cortical. What hymn? A, in this, is a big, big writing. The number, another powder for productivity, a pill out of a pretty tusk. To work with programmable data. I doubt the numbers relate to the productivity of attitude, of the down slope, during the buildup of which one hundred workers sang "The Mental Unorthodox!" a hymn of the phenomenal 20th century, the story of a little hard-working Patricia. Now, a little of the hymn:

"To be what you name/ know about productivity/ Later without refinancing/ I'm in the show/ But it's not about me// The looking up to authority/ To be different/ Belonging to a magnetic field/ I became recalled// Something like the applicable/ A ground-breaking theory/ To buy the ephemera/ Of the book about know-how/ That right to conduct/ Of that right conduct// Indictment over implement/ All magnetic fields/ To be a beautiful, critical welcomer/ To what you thought you departed/ Well, that, I think, a united right will do!"

Military officials certainly fell for her cheek. For her undergone. Apparently, he and fate conservatively rise in alliance to your Canadiana. Maybe they consult her first and make humanlike leaders meet face-to-face in the weave of gay marriage. He personally halted himself yesterday, called himself a particular 'particular' force. This is the new Martin: "Since I steal a lot perfectly, here in the party, leave me only a book I mailed once, and some gin. Rawl what you will, hours later, like to play. Lean to me, to meet, to metre." The spokesmen for the former alliance party leaders are baffled.

EASY TO NEW MECHANICAL KIDNEY ON ME!

The tower examples itself; the cultural stillness; a cluster of cities think to impact my end; the complete success story comes from a metamorphosis in its containers. I sat to encourage a simile. An A in finance is unknown. To see on and she inhaled me, I think. Everything he wills now, and primarily, and how he thinks to take many towers when he gets to thinking. Onto the speech, believe the range and saying snow, food for a little selling falls. Of necessity: its me.

Once established, the book's little son demonstratively lost his influence on the future as he was the one who had historically decided who held onto their instruments at the end of the orchestra. And who went home.

People were interested in making money, and for a time it turned out to be very successful hawking vacuums door to door; typically a project in small towns for a selection of the generation of writers who hasten to academic vacancies in a vain attempt to survive the woodlands of Canada: A text compatible with general foods: Come for the Indonesia, stay for sushi. I found it impossible to form an independent company of sentences, believing a paragraph should be forged as a corporate body out of the emotional data. Emotional data becomes legislation that incorporates the guts to charge a distinguishing breakthrough in published books that postpone ideology. I will just watch the victorious books by Canadian authors barb him offensively.

The defendant moved into the book at this point. He was an accountant who withdrew between a blue food bin and an overheated wonder of a red tractor. The overheated tractor and I dictated the extremely wonderful New York City snowfall of words that crackled your security review in wake of CBC media analysis.

We want thirty-six thousand dollars to fulfill the same Ontario cleansing commission, along the letters to unification, or Manitoba gets it. Small though the explosion was, it killed two Canadian soldiers. And out comes that last cigarette. The week is halted at Monday. West Hillhurst will separate if our demands are not met.

You become a in the it. We was owned by the bloodshed of failure. To place the cross where they thought the church gave poetry readings to young people who graduated from feeding liberal arts programs into the department called progress. Intelligent and 21, they were quite formed out of the preliterate masses and a frozen food culture of dramatic and litigious voices.

Terrorism became an idea that a and b could contribute to a world economy where a and b are both functions of the state. The understood delay in which we sell, as a humble welcome, the proffered black TWA building largely because it was going anyway.

Of which, I indicated, among other things, that she was in charge to conduct the collateral damage to be done to wild things, the coyotes and wolves, the wombats and spiders, etc. To be partial to the right, to compel the Western 21st century! She usually says: "Well the economy of time, to the ethical man, is a breakthrough used in underdeveloped countries as an unrelenting unit conducted among the people." But success in the Middle East was level with what one White House person had to say: "Well, among other things, we have a strong impact on the development of development. The country's net income rose in our diagnostic charts with legitimate wildlife in a directly connected relationship to the data without having the 55-year-old British writing company let you build a mockery of their jewels. With my play called *the alternate to the used*, game theory becomes inapplicable to conducting my best experiments to show that diphtheria proved useful in the field."

Inside their lungs are pounds of ash. Once a little Spokane was so medical that it would follow you north. Ill with the pro, you will him away in the reader, to destroy him a bit. Well-formed poems in the church will usually have you down to the punctuation. A whole in the old problem, worn into a the. Well, we have been quite quiet, who have to go now with you. Will him to a him to all you will I will he will a. Good night.

ACKNOWLEDGEMENTS

Canada Post would not have been possible without the many teachers and friends I've been fortunate to have had over the last few years. Of this category are: Chris Dewdney, Steve McCaffery, Nicole Markotic, Bruce Powe, Margo Swiss, Shyam Silvadurai, Richard Teleky and Fred Wah. Thank you all for your kindness, generosity and support.

I am indebted to my friends, especially former members of WAY, for consistently teaching me better ways in which to live. These luminaries are: John Barlow, derek beaulieu, Michael deBeyer, Christian Bök, Kyle Buckley, Louis Cabri, Natalee Caple, Maria Erskine, Chris Ewart, Jim and Alison and Ava Fay, Brendan Fernandes, Jon Paul Fiorentino, ryan fitzpatrick, Jill Hartman, Bill Kennedy, Paul Kennett, Frances Kruk, Larissa Lai, Sandy Lam, Jeremy Leipert, mmc, Jeremy Macleod, Rajinderpal S. Pal, angela rawlings, Rob Read, Andre Rodrigues, Sharanpal Ruprai, Andrea Ryer (love), Ian Samuels, Jordan Scott, Natalie Simpson, dw=h.

And thank you to my family for understanding the distances I've had to travel.

MARQUIS
MEMBER OF SCABRINI GROUP
Québec, Canada
2006